Why do whales sing?

Disney BOOKS BY MAIL

DK Direct Limited
Managing Art Editor Eljay Crompton
Senior Editor Rosemary McCormick
Writer Alexandra Parsons
Illustrators The Alvin White Studios and Richard Manning
Designers Amanda Barlow, Wayne Blades, Veneta Bullen,
Richard Clemson, Sarah Goodwin, Diane Klein, Sonia Whillock

The baby chimp on page 14 is a rescued chimp and
is being hand raised by Jim Cronin of
Monkey World, Dorset, England.

Contents

Do fish talk?

In a way, they do. They tell each other how they feel by the way they wiggle and blow bubbles. They also take in information about the world around them through their senses of sight, smell, touch, and taste – just like we do!

Fish talk
What two fish do you need to make a shoe?
A sole and an eel!

4

Glow on!

The fish who live down at the very bottom of the ocean have a special way of communicating. They glow with a bright light! Some light up to startle their prey, others just to say hello to each other.

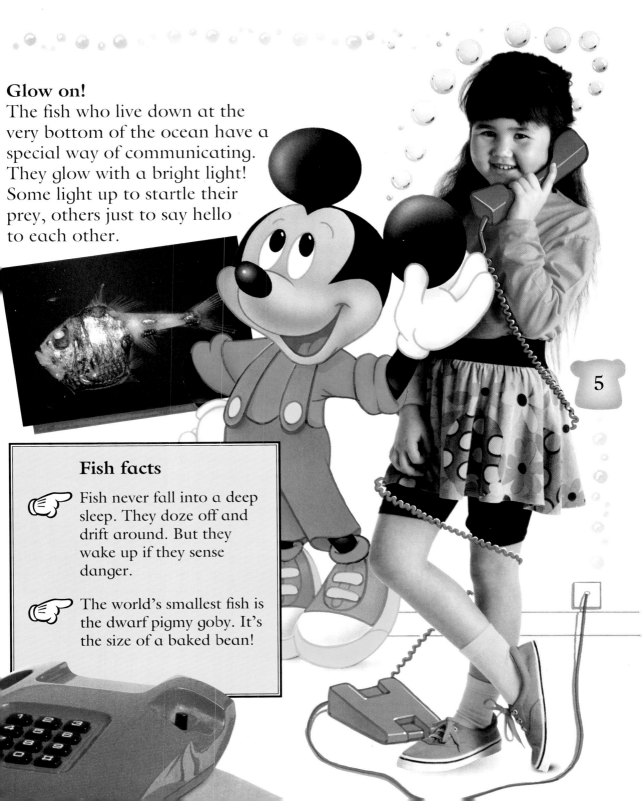

Fish facts

☞ Fish never fall into a deep sleep. They doze off and drift around. But they wake up if they sense danger.

☞ The world's smallest fish is the dwarf pigmy goby. It's the size of a baked bean!

5

Why do lions roar?

To tell visitors that they are not welcome! They are warning other lions to stay away from their territory. If there are too many lions in one place, there will not be enough food to go around.

6

Mother's work is never done!

The moms look after the babies and do all the hunting, while the dads prowl around and roar a lot.

Life of a lion

☞ Lions live in family groups called prides.

☞ They spend 20 hours a day resting or sleeping. That means they're only busy for four hours a day!

☞ Lions are part of the cat family. Pet cats are the only members of the family that can live happily with people.

Why do snakes hiss?

To warn their enemies that they are about to pounce, as if to say – stay back! Snakes make a hissing noise by pushing air out of their lungs over a rough area in their mouths. Try pushing air out of your mouth with your teeth together and hear that hiss!

8

Cat warning!
When cats are angry, they arch their backs, their fur stands on end, and they hiss, too!

Sssome sssurprising sssnakes

☞ The smallest snake in the world is the West Indian thread snake, which is thinner than the lead in a pencil.

☞ The fattest and heaviest snake is the anaconda. It has a body as thick as a telephone pole and can weigh 350 pounds, which is almost as much as three grown-ups.

Snaky joke
First snake: "Are we poisonous?"
Second snake: "Why?"
First snake: "I've just bitten my lip!"

Snakes alive!
Air being pushed through any small hole makes a hissing sound. Don't worry, Mickey, that's not the sound of a deadly snake!

Why do whales sing?

Because they love to "talk" to each other! Whales sing to signal to other whales, and just to be friendly. Male humpback whales are the best singers. They love to sing so much that they sing their own special songs over and over again. Each whale song lasts for up to 35 minutes.

10

And now, a big round of applause!
The song of the humpback whale is a beautiful melody of low whistling sounds. A record was made of a humpback whale's song, and it became a hit single.

To the rescue!
Whales can get trapped by ice. But the good news is, there are often people around to help them get back to the sea.

11

Whale facts

Whales only sing under water, but they sing very loudly. Their songs can be heard for hundreds of miles.

Blue whales are the biggest animals in the world. One adult blue whale weighs as much as 24 elephants. They can live to be 80 years old.

Why do peacocks have such beautiful tails?

To attract attention to themselves. Their long tail feathers turn into the most dazzling fans which make everyone stop and stare. Peacocks are male birds and they show off so that the females, called peahens, will think they look wonderful.

Show-off facts

Peacocks are members of the pheasant family.

When the peacock isn't showing off, his long tail feathers, called a train, trail along behind him.

An open peacock's train can be more than six feet high.

13

Ms. Peahen
Her feathers aren't as bright
and colorful as Mr. Peacock's!

How can you tell if a monkey is happy?

Because it will give you a lovely smile – showing only its bottom teeth. Monkeys show how they are feeling with their faces, just like we do. They smile when they are happy, frown when they are puzzled, and show all of their teeth when they are angry.

Happy families
Most monkeys live together in big families. This is a family grooming session. They like to keep each other nice and clean!

Monkey business

☞ Baby monkeys have to learn to walk just like human babies. A monkey mother will sit her baby down and walk away from it. Then she will encourage it to walk toward her.

☞ On the monkey's menu are berries, leaves, fruit, honey, and insects.

Top of the class! Chimpanzees are very clever. Some of them have even been taught to use sign language so they can ask politely for more bananas.

Can hummingbirds hum?

Yes, but not with their mouths the way people do. They use their wings instead. Hummingbirds flap their wings so fast that the wind they make creates a humming noise.

Home sweet home
Hummingbirds make cozy nests lined with soft fluff from plants and silky webs from spiders.

Little bitty birdy
The smallest bird in the world is the bee hummingbird. It's smaller than your thumb.

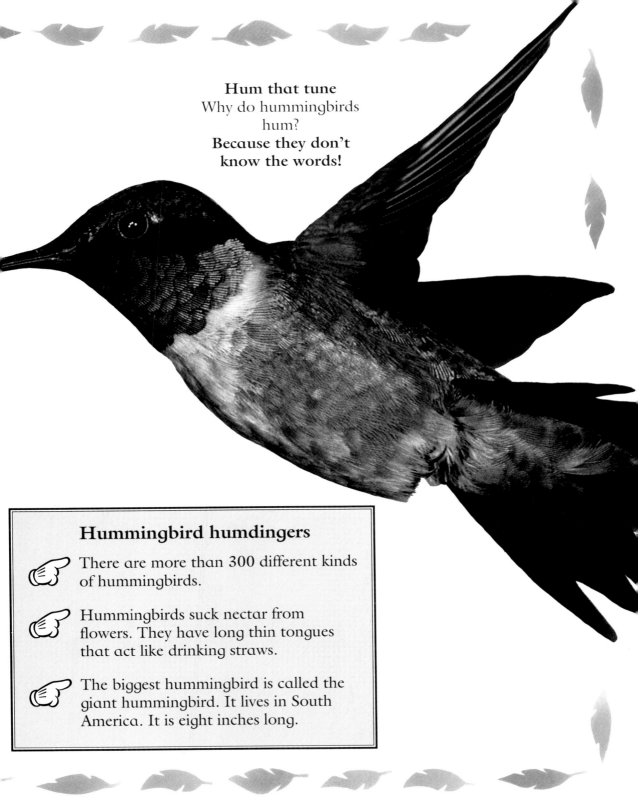

Hum that tune
Why do hummingbirds
hum?
**Because they don't
know the words!**

Hummingbird humdingers

There are more than 300 different kinds of hummingbirds.

Hummingbirds suck nectar from flowers. They have long thin tongues that act like drinking straws.

The biggest hummingbird is called the giant hummingbird. It lives in South America. It is eight inches long.

Do dolphins have a language of their own?

Yes, they do. They talk to each other by making whistling, squeaking, chirping, and clicking sounds. They make these noises by forcing air through flaps of skin just inside their blowholes.

In the swim!
Dolphins are very friendly. They like to swim with people and play games with them.

Dolphin facts

 Baby dolphins are born in the sea. They swim along next to their mothers.

 Dolphins live in all the seas of the world.

 Dolphins swim by moving their tail up and down.

Dolphins to the rescue!
Many tales have been told of
dolphins rescuing drowning
people by lifting them
gently on their backs
and carrying them
to shore.

Back to school
Dolphins swim
along together in
groups called
schools.

How do penguins know which babies are theirs?

Penguins may all look the same to us, but a mother and father penguin can pick out their chick on a crowded iceberg just by listening. To parents' ears, their chick's squawk sounds different from anybody else's.

Daddy shuffle
Father emperor penguin helps to take care of baby penguin while Mom goes off to the sea to eat. The baby snuggles next to Dad's tummy.

Hi, Mom!
Some baby birds, such as ducklings, will attach themselves to whatever they see when they first hatch. Sometimes it's their real mom and sometimes it isn't. Oh, dear!

Penguin facts

☞ There are 16 different kinds of penguins.

☞ Penguins are birds that cannot fly. They are expert swimmers and divers, though. The emperor penguin can dive as deep as 800 feet.

How do crickets chirp?

By rubbing their wings together. Male crickets have a rough area underneath their wings and a ridged part on top. When they rub these parts together they make music. Male crickets do this to say hello to lady crickets.

Built-in fiddle
The rough area underneath the wing is called the file, and the ridged area on top is called the scraper.

Chirpy cricket facts

☞ Some people say if you count the number of cricket chirps in 14 seconds, then add 40, it will give you the exact temperature.

☞ Crickets won't chirp if the temperature falls below 55°F.

☞ You can't always follow a cricket's chirp. It can make the noise seem like it's coming from someplace else.

It's been a long time!
Crickets, like this one, have
been around for millions
and millions of years. This
is the giant weta cricket
from New Zealand.

23

Does a giraffe have a voice?

Yes. But for such big animals, giraffes have very, very quiet voices. Mostly they grunt or bleat. Females moo quietly when they are hungry or when they are looking after their babies.

24

Wobbly legs
Adult giraffes grow to be 17 feet tall. But when giraffes are born, they are five feet tall, which is the height of a small grown-up.

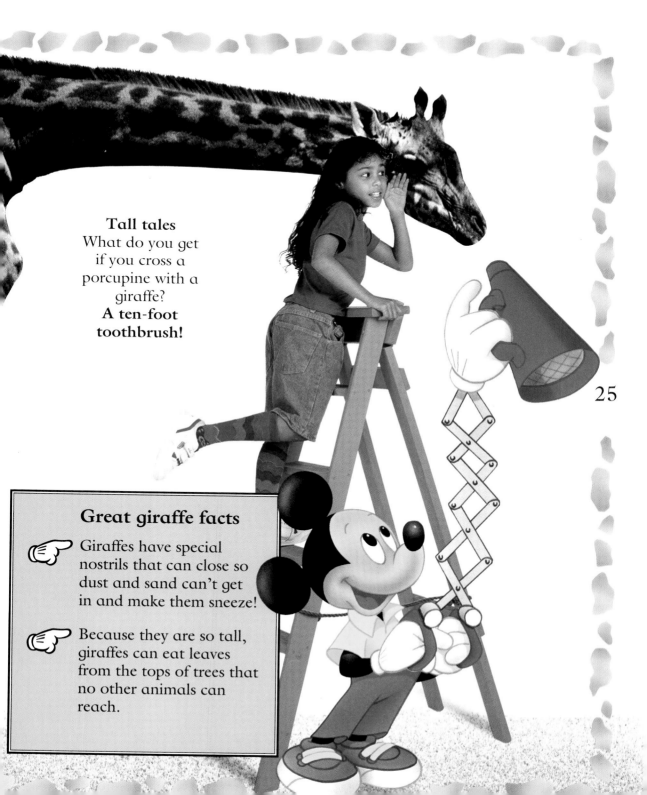

Tall tales
What do you get
if you cross a
porcupine with a
giraffe?
**A ten-foot
toothbrush!**

Great giraffe facts

Giraffes have special
nostrils that can close so
dust and sand can't get
in and make them sneeze!

Because they are so tall,
giraffes can eat leaves
from the tops of trees that
no other animals can
reach.

Why do bees dance?

To tell other bees where to find flowers filled with sweet nectar. Certain bees are sent out of the hive to look for flowers. Then they come back home and do a dance in the shape of a figure 8 to tell the other worker bees where to find the flowers. The bees will use the nectar to make honey.

Buzzy bee facts

☞ It takes nectar from 2,000 flowers to make one tablespoon of honey.

☞ Worker bees can fly at 15 mph, that's probably as fast as you can go on your bicycle.

☞ Most bees only sting to protect themselves.

Follow the sun

If you draw an arrow through the middle of the "8" in the direction of the sun, you'll find the nectar – if you're a bee that is!

Bee humor
What did the mother bee say to the naughty baby bee?
Beehive!

MICKEY'S Mind teaser

Animals talk without speaking.
Can you remember how these
animals "talk" to each other.